Thoughts from a Broken Mind

AF624696

Charlie Jessie

BookLeaf Publishing

Presentation by *BookLeaf Publishing*

Web: www.bookleafpub.com

E-mail: info@bookleafpub.com

ISBN: 9789357442848

First edition 2023

For my family and friends.

ACKNOWLEDGEMENT

I would like to thank:

My Mum and Dad for being so supportive and raising me to believe in myself and helping to inspire me with all that they do.

My sister Kirsty for listening to all of my first drafts and helping me edit them. And thank you for helping me pick a name for the book! Couldn't have done this without you.

My sister Zoë and sister-in-law Sam for giving me the courage to believe in my writing abilities and for always encouraging me to do what I enjoy. Thank you also for always listening to me and being there for me, you are truly amazing. And thank you for always listening to my drafts and giving me ideas.

My brother Steve and sister-in-law Kat and their kids Alice and Mike for being supportive of me.

My best friend Phoebe for being the ultimate best friend and for always being there for me through thick and thin.

Love you all so much!

And thank you to everyone at BookLeaf Publishing for making this dream come true!

PREFACE

Writing poems is not something that comes easily to me. I tend to edit my work a lot and spend an insurmountable amount time going over the words with a fine tooth comb, extracting the wrong words and replacing them with words that better suit the rhythm of the poem. Due to this way of writing, I rarely finish a poem before moving onto the next because, in my eyes, they are never finished. However there are some that I do complete, these tend to be put away, never to be seen again, which saddens me. So I decided to put them all together into this book, so that you can see them too.

I hope you enjoy reading them as much as I enjoyed writing them.

Disclaimer

The events that have been written about in this book are real and give a true representation of what the person went through, detailing their emotions. These are specific to the person and do not reflect all situations or feelings toward a certain subject matter.

Orange; A Haiku

The colour orange.
Brings forth light into my soul.
Kills the dark within.

Stars

Everyone has something in which they believe,
Mine is that we become stars when it's our time to leave.
Some may say it's silly or even naïve,
But souls becoming stars is not that hard to perceive.

Looking up at the stars is where I'd love to stay,
Talking up to them about what's happened in my day.
Science may say they're burning balls of gas so far away,
But that is not what I see when I look up to pray.

I find familial comfort when I bask in their glow,
Who is it I'm talking to? I always know.
They're my friends and family who left long ago,
Always there to listen to me, their love they always show.

Where do we go when our whole lives are through?
What do we see? What do we do?
I know where I'll be when my time is due,
I'll be in the sky, watching over you.

Voices

When night-time comes,
And I lie awake,
The voices appear,
And I start to shake.

They whisper all,
My deepest fears,
And scream so loud,
But I can't block my ears.

With their taunts,
Begging for a reply,
I try to ignore,
But still, I cry.

The familiar voice,
Inside my head,
It isn't mine,
And it fills me with dread.

The voice should comfort,
And tell me I'm fine,
But in my head, it scares me,
All of the time.

When dawn arrives,
And I still try to sleep,
The voices leave,
And I continue to weep.

When the voices have gone,
And I have to start my day,
Though I know they'll be back again,
I try to push the thought away.

- K-Lou

Joy

Through all my pain,
And the hardships of life,
There are some things,
That will always bring me joy.

Music soothes my soul,
And calms my mind,
It disperses my worries,
I listen all of the time.

Reading is something,
That I love to do,
Travelling to new locations,
And living a whole new life.

Sewing is a pleasure,
That I have always had,
Even though I struggle,
From my past experiences.

My family all around,
Is always a comfort,
Even though we sometimes fight,
I know they will always be there for me.

Through all my pain,
And the hardships of life,
These are some things,
That will always bring me joy.

- K-Lou

Looking At You Through The Glass

Looking in the mirror and all I see is you.
You look a lot like me, but I look nothing like you now.
You are so young, so pretty, so easily controlled,
So naïve, so weak, so easy to break.
Other eight-year-olds are laughing and playing,
Living their lives so carefree.
Yet you are nothing like them.
There's something going on in there, there's terror in your eyes.
I am helpless as I stand here watching the scene unfold,
The shadows growing darker in the place that you call home
I watch him approach from behind you,
Banging on the glass and screaming for you to run,
But my screams cannot be heard, and I'm stuck here forced to watch.
He asks to play a game, a game all eight-year-olds play;
He was twelve years old, so you followed his instructions.
"it's what all Mums and Dads do"

You did not know that this was not normal,
So you didn't seek help.
You knew that if you told, the others wouldn't believe you.
He was part of the family, he would never really hurt you.

Two years gone by, and still the same situation,
A little older now, knowing what's going on.
You try to confront him and tell him that it's wrong
Now not only are you scarred on the inside,
But also on the skin.
Still, I stand at the mirror, watching everything.
If I could break through this glass, I would come and rescue you,
I would crawl through the shards to come and take you far away
Somewhere you'll be safe and away from all this pain.
I would hold you in my arms and ensure that you are safe.
I would shush away your worries and chase away the fears.
Whilst in your world I would also pay a little visit
To the boy who thought all this was fun
I'd give him a taste of true frightening pain,

That way I could make sure that he never
touches you again.
Whilst I am with you, I would tell you
something true;
In the years to come you will make a difficult
choice
To save your heart and soul
You must choose to leave this life behind
Before you drown from the crashing waves of
family toxicity.

Looking in the mirror at my younger self
You're so beautiful on the outside, but so scarred
within.
You didn't understand that what he did was
wrong
I cannot come and save you, that is down to you
alone.
I wish I could tell you that time will heal all
wounds,
But the truth is you can never heal from
something this vile
You just learn to live with the feelings and the
triggers.
But sometimes you can surround yourself with
people who make it easier.
There are people out there who will help you
carry this weight

A family who will shine a light through the darkest of times.
“I promise you, it will get better”
I say to the little girl in the mirror.

-Anonymous

Fibonaccino

Dark
Ground
Coffee
Wake me up
Fill the void inside
Please make me productive today.

Be You

In a world where you can be anything...
Be Amazing
Be Beautiful
Be Caring
Be Daring
Be Empathetic
Be Freewheeling
Be Gentle
Be Honest
Be Inclusive
Be Jolly
Be Knowledgeable
Be Loving
Be Magnificent
Be Nice
Be Openminded
Be Positive
Be Quirky
Be Random
Be Self-Aware
Be Thoughtful
Be Unique
Be Valiant
Be Wonderful
Be Xenial

Be You
Be Zealous

"Why Didn't You Just Leave?"

People often ask "why didn't you just leave?"
She hated hearing this, for how could they just believe
that it would be so easy to simply just escape.
Don't you think it is time I told them how this story took its shape?

We start this story off with a fairy tale love,
The kind that gives one butterflies or feels like flying up above.
A burning new relationship still under construction.
Blissfully unaware that you would be her damned destruction.

Slowly though your personality started changing.
It was so palpable she could even feel you estranging.
One manic look spread across your face,
And the man she knew was gone, another stood in his place.

You became so controlling, so narcissistic,
At one point or another, you were even sadistic.
You basked in her pain, enjoying the 'glory'
But it is time someone told you, this whole thing was gory.

For a long time thereafter she did her best to try and leave
But your manipulations grew strong, they would make her believe.
You said that you loved her, and even promised to stop,
You said you'd get help, but secretly you did not.

She would stare up at the stars at night,
The only audience to this twisted sight.
She made them silent promises that you would never hear,
"I swear to you, someday I will get away from here!"

But when the daylight came, you were back to this,
One wrong word from her, from you another near miss.
Yet when she would try to say goodbye,
Your tears would come out and she'd believe a pretty lie.

People often say "why didn't you just leave?"
As though doing so is done with such ease.
How can she tell them what really transpired,
Every single time their relationship expired.

How can she tell them that she really did try,
But somehow every time, one would almost die.
Whenever she wanted to escape from your fist
You would hold up a knife against your own
wrist.

Mythology talks of a fatal flaw,
Hers is that she is loyal to the very core.
How could she ever leave you when you were
bleeding in her lap?
Even though she knew this was all some sordid
trap.

She really did believe there was only one way
out,
To commit a sinful act and watch her clock run
out.
She decided right then that she would rather take
flight
She packed her bag and drove away into the
night.

The stars up above, they saw it all,
From the very first kiss to the very last duel.
She never went back, and they never spoke
again
Her family has helped her heal from the pain.

It hurts to remember, but impossible to forget.
The time that she lived with this six-foot threat.
She is free now, she escaped at long last.
It has been so many years, you're just a man
from her past.

No matter what happened or what others may
say.
She swore it back then and still swears it to this
day.
There were two of you there in that body of
yours,
Fighting for control like a game of tug of wars.

Like a puppet on a string, she was pulled along.
Loved then abused, you did her so wrong.
Narcissistic behaviour, it is now known to be,
The way that you manipulated ME.

People often ask "why didn't you just leave?"
The right words to say, so painful to conceive.
So this is the answer if you really want to know.
Why it is so hard for some survivors to let go.

Roses Aren't Red

Roses aren't red,
They grow in all colours too.
Each colour has meaning
When gifted to you.

When roses are red,
They mean love and admiration.
When roses are purple,
They mean passion and infatuation.

When roses are pink,
It depends on the shade.
Light pink means sweetness and desire,
When gifted dark pink, gratitude is made.

When roses are yellow,
They mean friendship and cheerfulness.
When roses are white,
They mean heavenly innocence, bringing
tearfulness.

When roses are blue,
They mean unique and mysterious.
When roses are orange,
They mean enthusiasm, I'm serious.

Roses aren't red,
Sometimes they're green.
Look at the petals,
They'll show what they mean.

Sleep

Darkness surrounds and I succumB
Ethereal, like being thrown from afaR
Falling through the air, I try to breathE
Eventually feeling like I have had anaesthesiA
Numbing my mind. Not a thoughT
Enters my brain as I catch my breatH
Safely returning to a more secure leveL
Trying to regain my mental balancE
Reality trying to break through my
unconsciousnesS
Acutely aware of my surroundingS
This feeling in my braiN
Is like being thrown from a window up abovE
Offensively sudden, I regain consciousnesS
Never enjoying the feeling of Hypnagogic jerkS

PTSD

I retreat into myself to hide from the pain,
Of the bittersweet memories drowning my brain.
Need to get some oxygen, just breathe for heaven's sake.
Or from this frenzied state of mind, I shall never wake.

It's been so long. I feel like this should not affect me now.
Been told to 'get over it', but I really don't know how.
I feel so weak like this is not me.
Why can't these thoughts just let me be?

I put on a 'brave face' so no one can see me struggle,
All these memories in my brain, I'm trying hard to juggle.
Like water off a ducks back, I try not to let it in,
Putting on a fake smile, but it hurts like daggers within.

Don't want to 'play the victim', so to others, I never tell

When these flashbacks haunt my dreams and
make me so unwell.
Good times or bad, still so painful to relive,
Thoughts trespassing in my mind, I cannot
forgive.

Though heavy it may be, I carry it so well.
It doesn't break through the exterior, so others
cannot tell.
Mental health is stigmatised, by a lot of society,
But I think it's time we normalise these feelings
of anxiety.

Just because it doesn't match how someone else
is feeling,
Doesn't mean that anyone else can dictate how
my mind is healing.
Memories come crashing down like some
enormous wave,
I no longer need to hide away, I know that I am
brave.

Post Traumatic Stress Disorder can strike at any
time,
Days, weeks, months or years it does not have a
deadline.
But in order to heal from your time in the dirt,
You have to stop pretending that these feelings
do not hurt.

Waterfall

I long to be where the waterfall cascades,
It's so serene to watch and momentarily my
worry fades.
Being in this environment always makes me
smile,
Being one with nature makes the trek
worthwhile.
Watching a rainbow form is second to none,
When the mist of the water meets the hue of the
sun.
Being at the waterfall is where I long to be,
Especially when my family is enjoying it with
me.

City Vs Country

The city is loud, people bustling away.
The country is quiet and peaceful every day.
In the city, there are buildings that rise to the sky.
But in the country, it's mountains that sit way up high.
The city is so cramped, like walking through a maze
The country's scenery is empty, I could stare at it for days.
In the city, there is traffic and pollution from the cars.
In the country the sky is clear, you can see all the stars.
In the city, the air is so thick.
But out in the country, it heals you up quick.
Living in the city, I do truly miss.
But living in the country, I admit, is such bliss.

Home

On the outskirts of London
Is where I grew up,
With the people and places
That I always loved.

With always a thought
Of leaving that place,
To move somewhere new
Somewhere with more space.

A dream with my siblings
To live on a farm.
Way out in the country
Without any harm.

Now years have passed
Since we moved away,
From the place we once knew
And walked every day.

Even though
This place is not like
Where I grew up
And rode on my bike.

Not a day goes by
Where I don't regret
Leaving the city
And my old life behind.

The scenery is stunning
With the mountains in view.
I would love this kind of life,
Is what I always knew.

- K-Lou

Guest Limmerick

There was a young girl from surrey,
Who was always in a bit of a hurry,
She fell asleep in school,
And always looked cool,
And never gave a care or a worry.

-K-Lou

Platonic Soulmate

The phrase 'best friend' is a little seedy,
It doesn't quite capture what you mean to me.
You are so much more than that, in this poem you'll see,
Why 'platonic soulmate' is what suits you and me.

It was so long ago when we first met.
Your confidence was palpable, how could I forget?
I admit I was intimidated, but not by any threat.
I was awestruck by your personality, a beautiful asset.

School years flew by, we were like partners in crime,
As the final school bell started to chime.
A lifetime ahead, we began the steep climb
To see if our friendship would stand the test of time.

Different paths of life were led,
And the distance between us started to spread.
Being apart we both seemed to dread,
Worried we would start hanging by a thread.

Though the further apart we seemed to go
The closer and stronger our bond would grow.
There for each other through sun or snow.
A love never in question, we always know.

When we're together, we have so much fun.
A love like this is second to none.
You, the blue of the ocean, me the orange of the sun;
Belonging together beyond the horizon.

Good times and bad our bond will endure,
Through happy or sad, our love is always pure.
When one of us is down we always make sure
That the other is there like some sort of cure.

Though fights we've had so very few,
We always survive what we go through.
You're a part of me and I'm a part of you,
No matter what happens, I'll be here for you.

The phrase 'best friend' is still a little seedy,
It doesn't quite capture what it is that I see.
'Platonic soulmate' is what you are to me.
There is no one quite like you in the entire galaxy.
Forever and always I'll love you, Phoebe.

Ron

The once was a Tom Cat called Ron,
Who never thought he could do any wrong,
He meowed very loud,
And always looked proud,
And the love from his family was strong.

My Family

We grew up as six,
But new additions made us ten.
I love my big, crazy family;
So here's a silly poem about them.

But there is a little secret,
I have not said who's who!
So have some fun guessing
which stanza's about you.

You work so hard for us and have done all our lives.
I love you so much, but there's a thought I can't reserve,
I don't know if you know this, but you actually saved my life.
I think it's time you got the credit you so rightfully deserve.

You always answer when I call, no matter the time.
The first best friend I ever had, always by my side.
I love you so much for always being whatever it was I needed,

With the unconditional love that I know you'll
always provide.

Your dad jokes are so bad, I'm sorry but it's true,
But I know I would miss them, so please don't
ever stop.
Thank you for always being so caring when it's
needed.
When it comes to silly siblings, you're definitely
at the top.

You're so lovely and so caring, though a potty
mouth you have.
I know you don't hear it often, but you're a great
mother duck.
Keep doing what you're doing and know that
you are loved.
To have such lovely ducklings, you must have
some serious luck.

A little aspiring artist with long blonde hair and
big brown eyes.
Your personality is bubbly and so very funny.
Like Alice in Wonderland, you're in your own
little world.
But any day spent with you is so magical and
sunny.

A crazy little man running at 100 miles per hour.
You never slow down, you never sit still.
You're a tiny little terror to anyone who knows you.
But to have you any other way would be a major buzzkill.

You are very slightly mad and definitely unique.
Always there for me, even when I'm being mean.
You are truly very lovely, though I know you often doubt.
A true unbreakable bond we share, just like Sam and Dean.

We sometimes argue, but that's alright, I think because we're so alike,
We're always there for one another, even if we've lost our way.
You've been through so much, but still so brave, my favourite Lil bro.
You're always holding so much stress, but darling, you'll be okay.

You are truly really funny, and we have a great rapport.
A perfect peachy sister, that is what you are to me.

The others do not know what they are missing out on.
Not an original family member, but henceforth you will always be.

This is a silly little poem,
About my family,
I love them all like crazy,
And I know they all love me.

Grandad

Shadows were looming over you,
But just one was here to stay.
Alzheimer's had a grip on you
Getting tighter day by day.

You did so much, led an amazing life,
Looking after family is what you'd always do.
And so during your mental strife,
We did the same for you.

Barely touching reality,
Memories drifting so far away.
Though you lost who you used to be,
Our love for you would never sway.

We lost you twice in a way,
but in the stars, you were found.
When I look up to the sky to pray,
I feel your presence all around.

I talk to you at night, even though you don't talk back,
But everything is okay, you can rest where you are,
To me, you are in the sky, part of the zodiac.

I know that when I need you, I can wish upon a star.

When you left us, I was emotionally scarred.
But I'll try not to shed another tear y'know.
Saying goodbye is always hard,
But if there's one thing left to say, Grandad, I guess it's Cheerio!

Nan

Nan, why did you have to leave us,
our loving family?
We had many wonderful times together,
which will now live in our memory.

You gave us many treasures in life,
some were big while others small.
But to have you as our Nan,
was the greatest gift of all.

When your wings were ready,
we were not.
But as long as you live in our hearts,
you will never be forgot.

We did not want to lose you, Nan;
but you did not go alone.
Because a part of us went with you,
the day that Heaven called you home.

I now know why you left us, Nan;
our loving family.
Grandad needed you back with him,
and so, in our hearts, you will always be.

www.ingramcontent.com/pod-product-compliance
Lightning Source LLC
Chambersburg PA
CBHW051745130826
49812CB00033B/1015
9789357442848